WOK

© 1998 Rebo International b.v., The Netherlands
1998 Published by Rebo Productions Ltd.
Designed and created by Consortium, England

Original recipes and photographs on pages 8-9, 12-13,
22-23, 28-29, 44-45, 46-47, 48-49, 50-51, 52-53, 56-57
58-59, 68-69, 70-71, 72-73, 86-87 © Ceres Verlag,
Rudolf-August Oetker KG, Bielefeld, Germany
All other recipes and photographs © Quadrillion Publishing Ltd,
Godalming, Surrey GU7 1XW

Typeset by MATS, Southend-on-Sea, Essex
Cover design by Minkowsky, Buro voor grafische vormgeving
Enkhuizen, The Netherlands

Edited by Anne Sheasby
Ceres Verlag recipes compiled and translated by Stephen Challacombe
Illustrations by Camilla Sopwith

J0238UK
ISBN 1 84053 105 3

Printed in Slovenia

WOK

*Colourful, spicy and speedy
stir-fries, deep-fries and braised dishes*

REBO
PRODUCTIONS

Contents

Introduction

Cooking with a wok can bring about a revolution in your kitchen and a change in attitude to the foods you buy. This simple, inexpensive piece of equipment offers all sorts of possibilities for one-pot cooking. Although the wok is customarily used for stir-frying, it can also be employed for deep-frying, steaming and braising. Wok cooking not only saves on fuel and time, but it also cuts down on the washing up!

Stir-frying with a wok allows small pieces of food to be cooked in the minimum amount of oil over intense heat in just a few minutes. In this way, stir-fried dishes are healthily low in fat, but also the juices and flavours of the ingredients are sealed in so that their nutritional content is retained. The colours and textures of fresh vegetables are also preserved, which gives added encouragement to seeking out the youngest, most tender ingredients to enjoy in all their glory.

Traditional woks are made from carbon steel, which is a good conductor of heat. But these woks need to be oiled between use to prevent rusting, so be sure to follow the manufacturer's instructions. Stainless steel or aluminium woks do not need seasoning in the same way, but they do not heat up as efficiently as the carbon steel variety.

Just a few tips on using your wok. When stir-frying, always heat the wok before adding the oil. Have all your ingredients assembled and ready to use before you begin cooking, since time is of the essence! Cut ingredients into thin, evenly sized slices or small pieces to ensure even cooking. Partially freeze meat and poultry before slicing to make the job easier, and cut across the grain to retain tenderness during cooking. Add a small amount of food to the wok at a time, and cook in batches if necessary. When deep-frying, heat the oil without the lid on. Make sure that the wok is safely and securely positioned when containing hot oil.

Although the wok is chiefly used in Oriental cooking, it can also be used for cooking a whole variety of dishes. Here we present a selection of exciting, contemporary recipes for everyday meals and special occasions – some Thai and Chinese in style, some Indian in origin and others more recognisably Western. Whatever the dish, you will love the results of wok cooking!

Layered Bean Curd

An unusual but delicious way of serving bean curd (tofu).

Preparation time: 20 minutes, plus 15 minutes marinating time • Cooking time: 6-8 minutes • Serves: 4

Ingredients

50 g (1¾ oz) canned water chestnuts, drained	5 ml (1 tsp) salt
100 g (3½ oz) shrimps or prawns	15 ml (1 tbsp) potato flour, plus extra for sprinkling
100 g (3½ oz) minced pork	5 ml (1 tsp) finely chopped root ginger
30 ml (2 tbsp) finely chopped spring onions	500 g (1 lb 2 oz) bean curd (tofu)
10 ml (2 tsp) sesame oil	1 egg
30 ml (2 tbsp) rice wine	125 g (4½ oz) plain flour
5 ml (1 tsp) sugar	1 litre (1¾ pints) vegetable oil

Method

1

Thinly slice the water chestnuts, then place in a blender or food processor with the shrimps or prawns, pork and spring onions, and blend until smooth. Remove and set aside.

2

Mix the sesame oil, rice wine, sugar, 2.5 ml (½ tsp) salt, potato flour and ginger in a bowl to form a marinade. Add the purée, stir to mix and set aside to marinate for 15 minutes.

3

Rinse the bean curd and pat dry with absorbent kitchen paper. Cut the bean curd into 4 pieces crossways and cover with the purée. Sprinkle with extra potato flour to help the pieces bind together, then assemble the pieces and press together firmly.

4

In a bowl, mix together the egg, flour and 60 ml (4 tbsp) water and add 2.5 ml (½ tsp) salt. Heat the oil in a wok until hot. Coat the filled bean curd with the flour mixture, then lower slowly in a frying basket or slotted spoon into the hot oil and cook for 1 minute. Leave to fry in the oil for a further 5-7 minutes. Drain the bean curd thoroughly, cut into 4 portions and serve hot.

Serving suggestion

Serve with a mixed leaf side salad.

Variations

Use minced chicken or beef in place of the pork. Use garlic in place of fresh ginger. Use dry sherry in place of the rice wine.

Potato Pakoras

These spice-coated crunchy potato slices are easy to make, and can be served as a starter or a snack.

Preparation time: 15 minutes • Cooking time: 20 minutes • Serves 4-6

Ingredients

55 g (2 oz) gramflour or chick pea flour	½ tsp (2.5 ml) chilli powder
15 ml (1 tbsp) ground rice	50 ml (2 fl oz) water
2.5 ml (½ tsp) salt, or to taste	450 g (1 lb) medium-sized potatoes, peeled and cut into 5-mm (¼-inch) thick slices
7.5 ml (1½ tsp) ground coriander	
5 ml (1 tsp) ground cumin	Vegetable oil, for deep frying

Method

1

Place all the dry ingredients in a large bowl and stir to mix.

2

Add the water and mix to a thick paste.

3

Add the potatoes and stir until coated all over with the paste.

4

Heat the vegetable oil in a wok over medium heat, then add as many of the coated potato slices as the wok will hold in a single layer.

5

Fry the pakoras for 6-8 minutes, until golden brown.

6

Drain on absorbent kitchen paper and keep hot while cooking the remaining pakoras. Serve.

Serving suggestion

Serve with wedges of fresh ripe tomatoes and slices of cucumber.

Variations

Use sweet potatoes in place of standard potatoes. Use semolina in place of ground rice.

Cook's tip

Do not overcrowd the wok, otherwise the pakoras will stick together.

Pork and Seaweed Soup

A tasty combination of tender pork and seaweed served in a flavourful stock.

Preparation time: 15 minutes • Cooking time: 1 hour 5 minutes • Serves: 4

Ingredients

2 leaves dried tender seaweed	*125 ml (4 fl oz) rice wine*
600 g (1 lb 5 oz) neck of pork	*125 ml (4 fl oz) coconut milk*
2 litres (3½ pints) meat stock	*10 ml (2 tsp) salt*
10 g (¼ oz) root ginger, peeled and sliced	

Method

1

Soak the dried seaweed in about 1 litre (1¾ pints) water for 10-20 minutes, then remove and chop or shred. Set aside.

2

Meanwhile, rinse the pork under cold running water, pat dry, then cut into bite-sized pieces.

3

Place the stock in a wok and bring to the boil. Add the ginger, then add the meat, cover and simmer for about 1 hour, until cooked and tender, stirring once or twice.

4

Add the seaweed, rice wine, coconut milk and salt, stir to mix and cook for a further 5 minutes before serving. Ladle into bowls and serve hot.

Serving suggestion

Serve with crackers or fresh bread.

Variation

Use beef or chicken in place of the pork.

Nargisi Kababs

These spicy egg-filled meat kababs are quickly and easily fried in the wok.

Preparation time: 40 minutes • Cooking time: 10-15 minutes • Makes: 14 kababs

Ingredients

For the filling:	
2 hard-boiled eggs, shelled and coarsely chopped	7.5 ml (1½ tsp) ground coriander
1 fresh green chilli, seeded and finely chopped	5 ml (1 tsp) garam masala
30 ml (2 tbsp) finely chopped onion	2.5 ml (½ tsp) chilli powder
15 ml (1 tbsp) finely chopped fresh coriander	2.5 ml (½ tsp) freshly ground black pepper
1.25 ml (¼ tsp) salt	55 g (2 oz) thick set plain yogurt
15 ml (1 tbsp) set plain yogurt	15 ml (1 tbsp) chopped fresh mint or 5 ml (1 tsp) dried or bottled mint
25 g (1 oz) ghee or unsalted butter	30 ml (2 tbsp) chopped fresh coriander
1 large onion, chopped	5 ml (1 tsp) salt, or to taste
3-4 cloves garlic, peeled and chopped	550 g (1 lb 4 oz) lamb or beef mince
2.5-cm (1-inch) piece root ginger, peeled and chopped	1 egg
5 ml (1 tsp) ground cumin	30 ml (2 tbsp) gramflour or chick pea flour, sieved
	1 litre (1¾ pints) vegetable oil

Method

1

Combine all the ingredients for the filling in a bowl, mix thoroughly and set aside.

2

To make the kababs, melt the ghee or butter in a frying pan over a medium heat and fry the onion, garlic and ginger for 3-4 minutes. Reduce the heat, add the cumin, ground coriander, garam masala, chilli powder and black pepper and stir to mix. Fry for 1-2 minutes, stirring. Remove from the heat and set aside to cool.

3

Place the yogurt in a blender or food processor, add the fried ingredients, mint, fresh coriander, salt and mince. Blend until smooth. Transfer to a bowl.

4

Divide the mixture into about 14 golf ball-sized portions. Make a depression in the centre of each ball and form into a cup shape. Fill each with 1 heaped teaspoon of the egg mixture and cover the filling by pressing the edges together. Roll gently between the palms to form a neat ball, press the ball gently and form a round flat cake about 8-cm (¾-inch) thick. Make the rest of the kababs in the same way.

5

To make the batter, beat the egg and gradually add the gramflour or chick pea flour while still beating. Add 15 ml (1 tbsp) water and beat again.

6

Heat the oil in a wok over a medium heat. Dip each kabab in the batter and fry in a single layer without overcrowding the wok for 3-4 minutes on each side, until brown on both sides. Drain on absorbent kitchen paper and keep hot while cooking the remaining kababs. Serve hot.

Serving suggestion

Serve on a bed of crisp shredded lettuce with fresh tomato and cucumber slices.

Variation

Use chicken or turkey mince in place of the lamb or beef mince.

Meat Samosas

Serve these parcels of spiced minced meat with a mixed salad.

Preparation time: 50 minutes, plus cooling time • Cooking time: 15 minutes • Makes: 18 samosas

Ingredients

For the filling:

30 ml (2 tbsp) olive oil

2 medium-sized onions, finely chopped

225 g (8 oz) lean lamb or beef mince

3-4 cloves garlic, crushed

1-cm (½-inch) piece root ginger, finely grated

2.5 ml (½ tsp) ground turmeric

10 ml (2 tsp) ground coriander

7.5 ml (1½ tsp) ground cumin

2.5-5 ml (½-1 tsp) chilli powder

2.5 ml (½ tsp) salt, or to taste

175 g (6 oz) frozen peas

30 ml (2 tbsp) desiccated coconut

5 ml (1 tsp) garam masala

1-2 green chillies, finely chopped

30 ml (2 tbsp) chopped fresh coriander

15 ml (1 tbsp) lemon juice

For the pastry:

225 g (8 oz) plain flour

55 g (2 oz) ghee or butter

2.5 ml (½ tsp) salt

75 ml (2½ fl oz) warm water

Vegetable oil, for deep frying

Method

1

To make the filling, heat the oil in a frying pan over a medium heat, add the onions and fry until lightly browned.

2

Add the mince, garlic and ginger. Stir and fry until all the liquid evaporates, stirring frequently. Reduce the heat to low.

3

Add the turmeric, ground coriander, cumin, chilli powder and salt. Fry until the mince is lightly browned, stirring occasionally.

4

Add 125 ml (4 fl oz) water and the peas, bring to the boil, cover and simmer for 25-30 minutes, stirring occasionally.
If there is any liquid left, remove the lid and cook the mince over a medium heat until completely dry, stirring frequently.

5

Stir in the coconut, garam masala, green chillies and fresh coriander. Remove from the heat, stir in the
lemon juice and set aside to cool thoroughly.

6

To make the pastry, place the flour in a bowl, add the ghee or butter and salt and rub in lightly until the mixture resembles
breadcrumbs. Add the water and mix to make a soft dough. Knead until the dough feels smooth.

7

Divide the dough into 9 balls. Rotate each ball between your palms in a circular motion, then press down to make a flat cake.
Roll out each flat cake into 10-cm (4-inch) rounds and cut into 2. Use each semicircle of pastry as 1 envelope.

8

Moisten the straight edge with a little warm water. Fold each semicircle of pastry in half to form a triangular cone.
Join the straight edges by pressing them firmly together.

9

Fill the cones with the filling, leaving about a 5-mm (¼-inch) border on top of the cone.
Moisten the top edges and press firmly together.

10

Heat the oil in a wok until hot. Deep fry the samosas over a gentle heat until they are golden brown, then drain on absorbent
kitchen paper. Keep hot while cooking the remaining samosas. Serve hot, garnished with sprigs of fresh flat-leafed parsley.

Fish Tempura

This is a traditional Japanese dish, which can also be served as a unusual starter.

Preparation time: 30 minutes • Cooking time: 15 minutes • Serves: 4

Ingredients

12 uncooked whole king prawns	*1 egg yolk*
2 white fish fillets, skinned and cut into 5 x 2-cm (2 x ³/₄-inch) strips	*240 ml (8¹/₂ fl oz) iced water*
	Vegetable oil, for frying
Small whole fish, e.g. smelt or whitebait	*90 ml (3 fl oz) soy sauce*
2 squid, cleaned and cut into strips 2.5 x 7.5-cm (1 x 3-inch) long	*Finely grated rind and juice of 2 limes*
	50 ml (2 fl oz) dry sherry
115 g (4 oz) plain flour, plus 30 ml (2 tbsp) for dusting	

Method

1

Shell the prawns, leaving the tails intact. Wash the fish and squid, and pat dry with absorbent kitchen paper. Dust the seafood, fish and squid with the 30 ml (2 tbsp) flour.

2

Make a batter by beating together the egg yolk and water in a bowl. Sieve in the remaining flour and mix well.

3

Dip each piece of fish into the batter, shaking off any excess.

4

Heat the oil in a wok to 180°C/350°F. Lower in the fish pieces a few at a time and cook for 2-3 minutes. Using a slotted spoon, lift out carefully and drain on absorbent kitchen paper. Keep hot while cooking the remaining fish pieces.

5

In a bowl, mix together the soy sauce, lime rind and juice and sherry, and serve as a dip with the hot cooked fish.

Serving suggestion
Serve the fish tempura with the soy sauce dip alongside.

Variation
Use vegetables such as button mushrooms, courgettes and peppers in place of some of the fish.

Cook's tip
If the batter seems to drain off too quickly, leave each batch of fish in the bowl of batter until you are ready to lower them into the hot oil.

Steamed Fish Rolls

These fish rolls make a light, elegant dish – ideal for a special occasion.

Preparation time: 25 minutes • Cooking time: 10-15 minutes • Serves: 4

Ingredients

2 large sole or plaice, cut into 4 fillets	*5 ml (1 tsp) dry sherry*
175 g (6 oz) shelled prawns, chopped	*4 spring onions, green parts only, chopped*
10 ml (2 tsp) cornflour	*2 eggs, beaten with a pinch of salt*

Method

1

Skin the fish fillets carefully and lay them 'skin' side up on a flat surface.

2

In a bowl, mix the prawns with the cornflour, sherry and spring onions. Divide this mixture equally between the fish fillets and set aside.

3

Cook the eggs in a wok until softly scrambled. Spread equal quantities of the egg mixture over the prawn mixture.

4

Roll up the fish fillets swiss-roll fashion, folding the thicker end over first. Secure with wooden cocktail sticks.

5

Place a clean tea-towel in the bottom of a bamboo steamer and place the fish rolls on top. Cover and place over the wok filled with boiling water. Steam for 10-15 minutes, until the fish is cooked. Remove the cocktail sticks and serve immediately.

Serving suggestion

Serve with new potatoes and a fresh mixed salad.

Variations

Use shrimps or mussels in place of the prawns. Use rice wine in place of the sherry.

Cook's tip

Spread more of the filling towards the thicker end of the fillets, to help prevent it falling out as you roll.

Stuffed Seaweed Rolls

A quick and delicious way to serve seafood, wrapped in seaweed and deep-fried in the wok.

Preparation time: 20 minutes, plus 15 minutes marinating time • Cooking time: 15-20 minutes • Serves: 4

Ingredients

300 g (10½ oz) shelled king prawns	*Ground white pepper*
200 g (7 oz) salmon fillet	*5 ml (1 tsp) baking powder*
100 g (3½ oz) canned water chestnuts, drained	*4 leaves tender dried seaweed*
50 g (1¾ oz) spring onions, finely chopped	*1 litre (1¾ pints) vegetable oil*
10 ml (2 tsp) rice wine	*2.5 ml (½ tsp) ground Sichuan pepper*
7.5 ml (1½ tsp) salt	*2.5 ml (½ tsp) sugar*
15 ml (2 tsp) potato flour	*2.5 ml (½ tsp) crushed garlic*
30 ml (2 tsp) sesame oil	*2.5 ml (½ tsp) ground ginger*

Method

1
Clean and devein the prawns, wash under cold running water and pat dry with absorbent kitchen paper. Place in a blender or food processor and blend until smooth. Wash the salmon under cold running water and pat dry with absorbent kitchen paper. Cut into thin strips.

2
Thinly slice the water chestnuts. Add the salmon, water chestnuts and spring onions to the blender and blend until smooth. Place the mixture in a bowl.

3
In a separate bowl, mix together the rice wine, 5 ml (1 tsp) salt, potato flour, sesame oil, a little white pepper and baking powder. Add the puréed ingredients and mix well. Set aside to marinate for 15 minutes in a cool place.

4
Spoon about 60 ml (4 tbsp) of the blended mixture on each leaf of seaweed. Roll up lengthways, pressing the edges together to seal. Secure with cocktails sticks if you wish.

5
Heat the oil in a wok and fry each roll for about 3-4 minutes. Remove and set aside to cool slightly. Return each roll to the wok and fry for a further 1 minute, then drain, remove the cocktail sticks if using and slice each roll into 2-cm (¾-inch) rings.

6
Sprinkle the sliced rolls with Sichuan pepper, the remaining salt, sugar, garlic, ginger and 2.5 ml (½ tsp) white pepper. Serve with some of the remaining filling as a dip.

Serving suggestion
Serve with cooked fresh vegetables and boiled rice.

Variations
Use fresh tuna in place of salmon. Use shallots in place of the spring onions.

Prawns and Ginger

A nutritious, easy to prepare prawn dish with sweet and sour flavours.

Preparation time: 10 minutes • Cooking time: 8-10 minutes • Serves: 6

Ingredients

30 ml (2 tbsp) vegetable oil	*1 leek, white part only, cut into thin strips*
675 g (1½ lb) raw shelled prawns	*115 g (4 oz) fresh shelled peas*
2.5-cm (1-inch) piece root ginger, peeled and finely chopped	*175 g (6 oz) bean sprouts*
	30 ml (2 tbsp) dark soy sauce
2 cloves garlic, finely chopped	*5 ml (1 tsp) sugar*
2-3 spring onions, chopped	*A pinch of salt*

Method

1

Heat the oil in a wok, add the prawns and stir-fry for 2-3 minutes. Remove and set aside.

2

Reheat the oil and add the ginger and garlic. Stir quickly, then add the spring onions, leek and peas. Stir-fry for 2-3 minutes.

3

Add the bean sprouts and prawns to the cooked vegetables. Stir in the soy sauce, sugar and salt and stir-fry for 2 minutes. Serve immediately.

Serving suggestion

Serve on its own, or with boiled rice or egg noodles.

Variations

Use ready-prepared shrimps, shelled mussels or squid in place of the prawns. Use 1-2 celery sticks, finely chopped, in place of the spring onions.

Cook's tip

The vegetables can be prepared in advance and kept in airtight plastic boxes in the refrigerator for up to 6 hours before needed.

Prawns in Green Curry Paste

This is the hottest of Thai curries because of the large number of green Serrano chillies traditionally used in the Green Curry Paste.

Preparation time: 5 minutes • Cooking time: 10 minutes • Serves: 2

Ingredients

For the Green Curry Paste (makes 45-60 ml/3-4 tbsp):	
16 green Serrano or other small chillies, chopped	5 ml (1 tsp) ground nutmeg
3 cloves garlic, crushed	5 ml (1 tsp) shrimp paste
2 stems lemon grass, roughly chopped	45 ml (3 tbsp) vegetable oil
3 spring onions, chopped	200 ml (7 fl oz) thick coconut milk
5 ml (1 tsp) grated root ginger	30 ml (2 tbsp) Green Curry Paste
5 ml (1 tsp) coriander seeds	350 g (12 oz) raw shelled prawns
5 ml (1 tsp) caraway seeds	15 ml (1 tbsp) fish sauce
4 whole cloves	Pared or grated lemon rind, to garnish

Method

1

To make the Green Curry Paste, place the chillies, garlic, lemon grass and spring onions in a mortar and pound with a pestle until the mixture is well bruised and the juices begin to blend.

2

Add all the remaining ingredients except the oil and continue to pound until a paste is formed. Finally, blend in the oil.

3

Heat a little of the coconut milk in a wok and add the Green Curry Paste. Boil rapidly for 5 minutes, stirring frequently, then reduce the heat.

4

Gradually stir in the remaining coconut milk, then add the prawns and fish sauce. Cook gently for about 5 minutes, until the prawns are cooked. Garnish with lemon rind and serve immediately.

Serving suggestion

Serve with boiled rice or egg noodles.

Variation

Use ready-prepared squid or shelled mussels in place of the prawns.

Cook's tip

The Green Curry paste will keep up to 1 month in the refrigerator. Store in an airtight jar.

Squid with Spring Onions

Tender rings of squid served in a rice wine and soy-flavoured sauce.

Preparation time: 15 minutes, plus 20 minutes marinating time • Cooking time: 5-7 minutes • Serves: 4

Ingredients

350 g (12 oz) squid, body parts only, cleaned	**For the sauce:**
30 ml (2 tbsp) potato flour	10 ml (2 tsp) sugar
30 ml (2 tbsp) soy sauce	2 pinches of ground white pepper
30 ml (2 tbsp) sesame oil	5 ml (1 tsp) salt
250 g (9 oz) spring onions	75 ml (5 tbsp) vegetable stock
500 ml (18 fl oz) vegetable oil	75 ml (5 tbsp) rice wine
75 ml (5 tbsp) soya oil	5 ml (1 tsp) potato flour
5 ml (1 tbsp) finely chopped root ginger	30 ml (2 tbsp) sunflower oil
	5 ml (1 tsp) soy sauce

Method

1

Rinse the squid under cold running water, remove any outside skin and discard and cut into 5-mm (¼-inch) rings. Set aside.

2

Place the potato flour, soy sauce and sesame oil in a bowl and mix well. Add the squid, stir to mix, then set aside to marinate for 20 minutes. Clean and prepare the spring onions, cutting into 4-cm (1½-inch) pieces.

3

Heat the vegetable oil in a wok until hot, then fry the squid for about 1 minute. Remove and drain on absorbent kitchen paper. Set aside and keep hot. Pour the hot oil into a suitable heatproof container and set aside. Heat the soya oil in the wok, add the ginger and spring onions and stir-fry for 2-3 minutes.

4

To make the sauce, in a bowl mix together the sugar, white pepper, salt, stock, rice wine, potato flour, sunflower oil and soy sauce. Pour over the ginger and spring onions in the wok. Return the squid to the wok, stir-fry until cooked and piping hot, then serve immediately.

Serving suggestion
Serve with boiled rice or egg-fried rice.

Variations
Use raw shelled king or small prawns in place of the squid. Use thinly sliced leeks in place of the spring onions.

Chicken and Peanut Curry

This Thai dish is sometimes known as dry chicken curry because of its thick sauce.

Preparation time: 10 minutes, plus 1 hour marinating time • Cooking time: 15 minutes • Serves: 4

Ingredients

450 g (1 lb) chicken breasts, skinned and boned	1.25 ml (¼ tsp) ground coriander
Juice of 1 lemon	115 g (4 oz) roasted peanuts, ground
Juice of 1 lime	150 ml (¼ pint) chicken stock
3 green chillies, seeded and chopped	150 ml (¼ pint) thick coconut milk
60 ml (4 tbsp) sunflower or groundnut oil	85 g (3 oz) freshly grated coconut flesh
1 onion, chopped	15 ml (1 tbsp) sugar
1.25 ml (¼ tsp) ground cumin	15 ml (1 tbsp) fish sauce

Method

1

Cut the chicken into bite-sized pieces and place in a shallow dish. In a bowl, mix together the lemon juice, lime juice and chopped chillies and pour over the chicken. Toss together until the chicken is coated. Cover and set aside to marinate for 1 hour.

2

Heat the oil in a wok, add the onion and fry until softened and beginning to brown. Stir in the cumin and coriander. Remove the chicken from the marinade with a slotted spoon, add to the wok and stir-fry quickly until browned all over.

3

Add the marinade to the wok and stir-fry over a high heat for 2-3 minutes.

4

Stir in the ground peanuts, then gradually add the stock and coconut milk. Add the coconut flesh, sugar and fish sauce, then reduce the heat and simmer gently for 5 minutes, or until the chicken is cooked through, stirring occasionally. Serve immediately.

Serving suggestion

Serve with boiled jasmine rice.

Variations

Use crunchy peanut butter in place of the ground roasted peanuts. Use turkey or pork in place of the chicken.

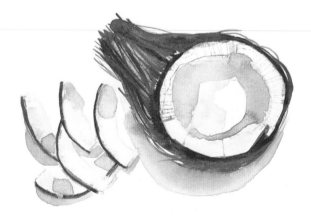

Sesame Chicken Wings

This is an economical dish and makes a satisfying light meal served with stir-fried vegetables.

Preparation time: 20 minutes • Cooking time: 15 minutes • Serves: 6-8

Ingredients

12 chicken wings	*45 ml (3 tbsp) soy sauce*
15 ml (1 tbsp) salted black beans	*22.5 ml (1½ tbsp) rice wine or dry sherry*
15 ml (1 tbsp) groundnut oil	*A large pinch of black pepper*
2 cloves garlic, crushed	*15 ml (1 tbsp) sesame seeds*
2 slices root ginger, peeled and cut into fine shreds	

Method

1

Cut off and discard the wing tips from the chicken. Cut between the join to separate into two pieces.

2

Crush the black beans and add 15 ml (1 tbsp) boiling water. Set aside to stand for a few minutes.

3

Heat the oil in a wok and add the garlic and ginger. Stir briefly, then add the chicken wings and stir-fry for about 3 minutes, until lightly browned. Add the soy sauce and wine or sherry and cook, stirring, for about a further 30 seconds. Add the soaked black beans and pepper.

4

Cover the wok tightly, reduce the heat and simmer for about 8-10 minutes. Uncover and increase the heat to high. Continue cooking, stirring, until the liquid is almost evaporated and the chicken wings are glazed with sauce. Remove from the heat and sprinkle with the sesame seeds. Stir to coat completely and serve. Garnish with spring onions or coriander, if you wish.

Serving suggestion

To garnish with spring onion brushes, trim the roots and green tops of spring onions and cut both ends into thin strips, leaving the middle portion intact. Place in ice water for several hours or overnight for the cut ends to curl up. Drain and use as a garnish.

Variations

Use poppy seeds in place of the sesame seeds. Use apple juice in place of the rice wine or sherry.

Cook's tip

You can prepare the chicken wings ahead of time and reheat them. They are best reheated in the oven for 10-15 minutes at 180°C/350°F/Gas Mark 4. Ensure that they are piping hot before serving.

Chicken and Cashew Nuts

This classic stir-fried Oriental dish offers a medley of interesting flavours and textures.

Preparation time: 15 minutes • Cooking time: 15 minutes • Serves: 4

Ingredients

350 g (12 oz) chicken breast, sliced into 2.5-cm (1-inch) pieces	1 small onion, diced
15 ml (1 tbsp) cornflour, plus 10 ml (2 tsp)	2.5-cm (1-inch) piece root ginger, peeled and finely sliced
5 ml (1 tsp) salt	2 cloves garlic, thinly sliced
5 ml (1 tsp) sesame oil	85 g (3 oz) mangetout
15 ml (1 tbsp) light soy sauce	55 g (2 oz) bamboo shoots, thinly sliced
2.5 ml (½ tsp) sugar	115 g (4 oz) cashew nuts
75 ml (5 tbsp) vegetable oil	15 ml (1 tbsp) hoisin sauce, or barbecue sauce
2 spring onions, chopped	250 ml (9 fl oz) chicken stock

Method

1
Roll the chicken pieces in the 15 ml (1 tbsp) cornflour. Reserve any excess cornflour.

2
In a large bowl, mix together the salt, sesame oil, soy sauce and sugar. Place the chicken in the marinade mixture and stir to mix. Cover and leave to stand in the refrigerator for 10 minutes.

3
Heat 30 ml (2 tbsp) vegetable oil in a wok, add the spring onions, ginger and garlic and stir-fry for 2-3 minutes.

4
Add the mangetout and bamboo shoots and stir-fry for a further 3 minutes.

5
Remove the fried vegetables and set aside. Add a further 15 ml (1 tbsp) oil to the wok and heat through.

6
Lift the chicken pieces out of the marinade and stir-fry in the hot oil for 3-4 minutes, until cooked through.

7
Remove the cooked chicken pieces, set aside and keep hot. Clean the wok.

8
Add the remaining oil to the wok, return the chicken and fried vegetables to the wok and stir in the cashew nuts.

9
Mix together the remaining cornflour with the hoisin or barbecue sauce and the chicken stock. Pour this over the chicken and vegetables in the wok and stir-fry over a moderate heat, until the ingredients are heated through and the sauce has thickened. Serve immediately.

Serving suggestion
Serve this stir-fry with a dish of boiled egg noodles.

Variations
Stir 85 g (3 oz) pineapple chunks into the stir-fry mixture just before serving. Use turkey or pork in place of the chicken. Use sugar-snap peas or sliced mushrooms in place of the mangetout.

Chicken with Cloud Ears

Cloud ears is the delightful name for an edible tree fungus which is mushroom-like in taste and texture.

Preparation time: 20 minutes • Cooking time: 10 minutes • Serves: 6

Ingredients

12 cloud ears, wood ears or other dried Chinese mushrooms	*2.5-cm (1-inch) piece root ginger, left whole*
450 g (1 lb) skinless, boneless chicken breasts, thinly sliced	*1 clove garlic, left whole*
1 egg white, beaten	*300 ml (½ pint) chicken stock*
10 ml (2 tsp) cornflour	*15 ml (1 tbsp) cornflour*
10 ml (2 tsp) white wine	*45 ml (3 tbsp) light soy sauce*
10 ml (2 tsp) sesame oil	*A pinch of salt and freshly ground black pepper*
300 ml (½ pint) vegetable oil, for deep-frying	*Spring onion brushes (see 'Serving suggestion', page 32), to garnish*

Method

1

Soak the mushrooms in boiling water for about 10 minutes, until they soften and swell. In a bowl, mix the chicken with the egg white, cornflour, wine and sesame oil.

2

Heat the wok for a few minutes and pour in the oil for deep-drying. Add the ginger and garlic clove, and cook for about 1 minute. Remove and discard, then reduce the heat.

3

Add about a quarter of the chicken at a time and stir-fry for about 1 minute. Remove and place on a plate, then continue cooking until all the chicken is fried. Remove all but about 30 ml (2 tbsp) of the oil from the wok.

4

Drain the mushrooms and squeeze to extract all the liquid. Discard the liquid. If using mushrooms with stems, remove the stems before thinly slicing. Cut cloud ears or wood ears into smaller pieces. Add to the wok and cook for about 1 minute.

5

Add the stock and allow it to come almost to the boil. In a bowl, mix together the cornflour and soy sauce, then add a spoonful of the hot stock. Add the mixture to the wok and bring to the boil, stirring continuously. Alow to boil for 1-2 minutes, or until thickened. The sauce will clear when the cornflour has cooked sufficiently.

6

Return the chicken to the wok and add salt and pepper to taste. Stir thoroughly for about 1 minute, then serve immediately garnished with spring onion brushes.

Serving suggestion

Serve with boiled rice, pasta or egg noodles.

Variations

Use pork or turkey in place of the chicken. Use red wine in place of the white wine.

Cook's tip

Dried cloud ears or wood ears are available from Chinese supermarkets and some delicatessens. Shiitake mushrooms are more readily available. Both keep a long time in their dried state.

Aubergine and Chicken Chilli

An exciting yet easy way to serve chicken, for a filling family supper dish.

Preparation time: 15 minutes, plus 30 minutes standing time • Cooking time: 15 minutes • Serves: 4

Ingredients

2 medium-sized aubergines	350 g (12 oz) skinless, boneless chicken breast, cut into thin slices
Salt	
60 ml (4 tbsp) sesame oil	30 ml (2 tbsp) chicken or vegetable stock
2 cloves garlic, crushed	15 ml (1 tbsp) tomato purée
4 spring onions, cut into thin diagonal strips	5 ml (1 tsp) cornflour
1 green chilli, finely chopped	Sugar, to taste

Method

1
Using a sharp knife, cut the aubergines into quarters lengthways. Slice the aubergine quarters into pieces approximately 1-cm (½-inch) thick.

2
Place the aubergine slices in a bowl and sprinkle liberally with salt. Stir well to coat evenly.
Cover with cling film and leave to stand for 30 minutes.

3
Rinse the aubergine slices very thoroughly under cold running water, then pat dry with a clean tea towel.

4
Heat half the oil in a wok, add the garlic and cook gently until soft but not coloured.

5
Add the aubergine slices to the wok and stir-fry for 3-4 minutes.

6
Stir the spring onions together with the chilli into the cooked aubergine, and stir-fry for a further 1 minute.
Remove the aubergine and onion mixture from the wok and set aside, keeping warm.

7
Heat the remaining oil in the wok, add the chicken pieces and stir-fry for about 2 minutes, or until thoroughly cooked.

8
Return the aubergine and onions to the pan and stir-fry for 2 minutes, or until piping hot.

9
Mix together the remaining ingredients and pour over the chicken and aubergines in the wok, stirring constantly, until the sauce has thickened and cleared. Serve immediately.

Serving suggestion
Serve as part of a full Chinese-style meal with boiled egg noodles.

Variations
Use lamb or beef in place of the chicken. Use 2 shallots, finely chopped, in place of the spring onions.

Cook's tip
The vegetables can be prepared well in advance, but the aubergines should be removed from the salt after 30 minutes, or they will become too dehydrated.

Chicken with Walnuts and Celery

Oyster sauce lends a subtle, slightly salty taste to this appetising Cantonese dish.

Preparation time: 15 minutes • Cooking time: 10 minutes • Serves: 4

Ingredients

225 g (8 oz) boned chicken, cut into 2.5-cm (1-inch) pieces	*30 ml (2 tbsp) groundnut oil*
	1 clove garlic
10 ml (2 tsp) soy sauce	*115 g (4 oz) walnut halves*
10 ml (2 tsp) brandy	*3 sticks celery, thinly sliced diagonally*
5 ml (1 tsp) cornflour	*10 ml (2 tsp) oyster sauce*
Salt and freshly ground black pepper	*150 ml (¼ pint) chicken stock*

Method

1

In a bowl, combine the chicken with the soy sauce, brandy, cornflour and salt and pepper.

2

Heat the wok and add the oil and garlic. Cook for about 1 minute to flavour the oil.

3

Remove and discard the garlic, then add the chicken in two batches. Stir-fry quickly without allowing the chicken to brown. Remove the chicken, place on a plate and keep hot. Add the walnuts to the wok and stir-fry for about 2 minutes, until slightly brown and crisp.

4

Add the celery to the wok and stir-fry for about 1 minute. Add the oyster sauce and chicken stock and bring to the boil. When boiling, return the chicken to the pan and stir to coat all the ingredients thoroughly. Serve immediately.

Serving suggestion
Serve with cooked fresh vegetables and boiled rice.

Variations
Use almonds or cashew nuts in place of the walnuts and add along with the celery. Use carrots in place of the celery.

Cook's tip
Nuts can burn very easily. Stir them constantly for even browning.

Chicken Liver Stir-Fry

Chicken livers are low in fat and high in flavour. They also require little cooking, so are perfect for stir-frying.

Preparation time: 20 minutes • Cooking time: 10 minutes • Serves: 4

Ingredients

450 g (1 lb) chicken livers	*8-10 Chinese leaves, shredded*
45 ml (3 tbsp) sesame oil	*10 ml (2 tsp) cornflour*
55 g (2 oz) split blanched almonds	*30 ml (2 tbsp) soy sauce*
1 clove garlic, peeled	*150 ml (¼ pint) chicken or*
55 g (2 oz) mangetout, trimmed	*vegetable stock*

Method

1
Trim the chicken livers, removing any discoloured areas or fatty tubes. Cut the livers into even-sized pieces and set aside.

2
Heat the wok and pour in the oil. When the oil is hot, reduce the heat, add the almonds and stir-fry until they are pale golden brown. Remove the almonds, draining any oil back into the wok. Set aside on absorbent kitchen paper.

3
Add the garlic clove to the wok and cook for 1-2 minutes to flavour the oil. Remove the garlic and discard.

4
Stir the livers into the flavoured oil and stir-fry for 2-3 minutes, to brown evenly.
Remove the livers from the wok, set aside and keep hot.

5
Add the mangetout to the hot oil and stir-fry for about 1 minute. Stir in the Chinese leaves and cook for 1 minute.
Remove the vegetables, set aside and keep hot.

6
In a bowl, mix together the cornflour and 15 ml (1 tbsp) cold water, then blend in the soy sauce and stock.

7
Pour the cornflour mixture into the wok and bring to the boil, stirring continuously until the sauce has thickened and cleared.

8
Return all other ingredients to the wok and heat through for 1 minute, until piping hot. Serve immediately.

Serving suggestion
Serve with fried rice or boiled egg noodles.

Variations
Use finely sliced lamb's or calf's liver in place of the chicken livers. Use spinach in place of the Chinese leaves.

Spicy Duck with Chillies

A delicious stir-fry of tender duck breast cooked and served in a hot, spicy sauce.

Preparation time: 10 minutes, plus 15 minutes marinating time • Cooking time: 10 minutes • Serves: 4

Ingredients

500 g (1 lb 2 oz) skinless, boneless duck breast	*45 ml (3 tbsp) rice vinegar*
75 ml (5 tbsp) light soy sauce	*45 ml (3 tbsp) oyster sauce*
15 ml (1 tbsp) potato flour	*45 ml (3 tbsp) dark soy sauce*
30 ml (2 tbsp) beaten egg white	*15 ml (1 tbsp) finely chopped root ginger*
45 ml (3 tbsp), plus 500 ml (18 fl oz) vegetable oil	*85 g (3 oz) spring onions, chopped*
30 ml (2 tbsp) groundnut oil	*5 fresh red chillies, cut into thin strips*
5 ml (1 tsp) cornflour	*Spring onion brushes (see 'Serving suggestion', page 32), to garnish*
45 ml (3 tbsp) rice wine	

Method

1

Rinse the duck under cold running water, pat dry with absorbent kitchen paper and thinly slice. For the marinade, in a bowl, mix together 30 ml (2 tbsp) of the light soy sauce, potato flour, egg white and 45 ml (3 tbsp) of the vegetable oil. Add the duck, stir to mix well, then set aside to marinate for 15 minutes.

2

Meanwhile, for the sauce, mix together the groundnut oil, the remaining 45 ml (3 tbsp) light soy sauce, cornflour, rice wine, rice vinegar, oyster sauce, dark soy sauce and 45 ml (3 tbsp) water in a bowl. Set aside.

3

Heat the remaining 500 ml (18 fl oz) of the vegetable oil in a wok, add the duck and cook for about 1 minute. Remove the duck and keep hot.

4

Pour off all but 75 ml (5 tbsp) oil, reheat, then add the ginger and stir-fry for 1 minute. Return the duck to the wok together with the spring onions and chillies and stir-fry for a further 2 minutes.

5

Pour in the marinade and sauce and stir-fry for about 1 minute, until piping hot. Serve immediately, garnished with spring onion brushes.

Serving suggestion

Serve with boiled jasmine rice.

Variations

Use chicken or pork in place of the duck. Use dry sherry in place of the rice wine.

Stir-Fried Breast of Duck

A simple stir-fry of duck, bean curd (tofu) and Chinese vegetables.

Preparation time: 15 minutes, plus 40 minutes soaking time • Cooking time: 10 minutes • Serves: 4

Ingredients

300 g (10½ oz) skinless, boneless duck breast	*30 ml (2 tbsp) light soy sauce*
200 g (7 oz) spinach leaves	*30 ml (2 tbsp) dark soy sauce*
3 Chinese mushrooms, soaked in cold water for 40 minutes and drained	*15 ml (1 tbsp) rice wine*
150 g (5½ oz) bean curd (tofu)	*5 ml (1 tsp) salt*
500 ml (18 fl oz) vegetable oil	*Freshly ground black pepper*
105 ml (7 tbsp) soya oil	*15 ml (1 tbsp) sugar*
1-2 cloves garlic, finely chopped	*7.5 ml (1½ tsp) potato flour*
	75 ml (5 tbsp) chicken stock

Method

1
Rinse the duck breast under cold running water, then blanch in a saucepan of boiling water for 3-5 minutes. Remove, set aside to cool, then cut into slices.

2
Prepare and wash the spinach, slice the mushrooms into chunks and cut the bean curd into bite-sized pieces.

3
Heat the vegetable oil in a wok, add the bean curd and fry for about 2 minutes. Remove and set aside. Tip the hot oil into a heatproof storage container.

4
Heat the soya oil in the wok, add the garlic, spinach, bean curd and duck breast, cover the wok and cook for about 1 minute.

5
For the sauce, stir the light soy sauce, dark soy sauce, rice wine, salt and pepper, sugar and potato flour into the chicken stock, add to the wok and stir-fry for about 2 minutes. Serve immediately.

Serving suggestion
Serve with egg-fried rice or noodles.

Variations
Use chicken or turkey in place of the duck. Use spring greens in place of the spinach. Use root ginger in place of the garlic.

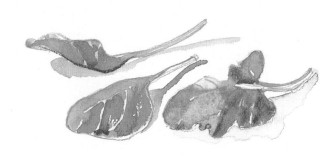

Crispy Duck

A flavourful adaptation of a classic Oriental dish.

Preparation time: 2 hours • Cooking time: 10 minutes • Serves: 4-6

Ingredients

1 duck, weighing 1.8-2 kg (4 lb-4 lb 8 oz)	5 ml (1 tsp) sambal oelek
1 litre (1¾ pints) vegetable oil	5 ml (1 tsp) vinegar
75 ml (5 tbsp) groundnut oil	2.5 ml (½ tsp) salt
3 cloves garlic, thinly sliced	15 ml (1 tbsp) sugar
100 g (3½ oz) mangetout, trimmed	45 ml (3 tbsp) soy sauce
55 g (2 oz) carrots, thinly sliced	30 ml (2 tbsp) rice wine
2 fresh red chillies, thinly sliced	5 ml (1 tbsp) potato flour
20 g (¾ oz) spring onions, cut into strips	

Method

1

Rinse the duck under cold running water and drain well. Place the duck in the wok and cover with 3 litres (5¼ pints) water. Bring to the boil and simmer, covered, for about 2 hours, or until the carcass begins to disintegrate.

2

Discard the water. Remove and discard the skin and bones from the duck, and break the flesh into very small pieces.

3

Heat the vegetable oil in the wok. Add the duck and stir-fry for 1 minute. Remove and drain, then fry the duck pieces again until golden brown and crispy. Remove the duck pieces, drain thoroughly on absorbent kitchen paper and set aside. Transfer the oil to a suitable heatproof container and set aside.

4

Heat the groundnut oil in the wok, add the garlic, mangetout, carrots and chillies and stir-fry for 1 minute. Add the spring onions and stir-fry for 1 minute.

5

Return the duck to the wok, add the sambal oelek, vinegar, salt, sugar, soy sauce and rice wine and stir-fry for 1 minute. Mix the potato flour with 45 ml (3 tbsp) water, add to the wok and stir-fry until thickened. Serve immediately.

Serving suggestion
Serve with boiled rice or egg noodles.

Variations
Use a chicken or a small turkey in place of the duck. Use parsnips in place of the carrots.

Pork Stir-Fry

Slices of pork stir-fried with carrots and served in a rich, slightly sweet sauce.

Preparation time: 10 minutes • Cooking time: 45 minutes • Serves: 4-6

Ingredients

500 g (1 lb 2 oz) boneless neck of pork	75 ml (2½ fl oz) soy sauce
200 g (7 oz) carrots	125 ml (4 fl oz) plum wine
500 ml (18 fl oz) vegetable oil	20 g (¾ oz) soft brown sugar
120 ml (8 tbsp) groundnut oil	500 ml (18 fl oz) hot meat stock
20 g (¾ oz) root ginger, peeled and sliced	5 ml (1 tsp) salt
5 ml (1 tsp) cornflour	Fresh herb sprigs, to garnish

Method

1

Wash the pork under cold running water, pat dry with absorbent kitchen paper, then cut into slices.
Slice the carrots and set aside.

2

Heat the vegetable oil in a wok, add the pork and stir-fry for about 2 minutes. Remove and drain on absorbent kitchen paper.
Set aside and keep hot. Transfer the oil to a suitable heatproof container and set aside.

3

Heat the groundnut oil in the wok, add the ginger and stir-fry about 1 minute. Roll the pork slices in the cornflour
and cover with soy sauce. Add to the wok a few at a time and stir-fry for 2 minutes per batch.
Place on a plate and keep hot while cooking the remaining pork.

4

Return all the part-cooked pork to the wok, add the carrots, cover and cook for 1-2 minutes.

5

Add the plum wine, sugar, stock and salt. Cover and cook for about 30 minutes, until the pork is cooked
and tender, stirring occasionally. Serve hot, garnished with fresh herb sprigs.

Serving suggestion
Serve with boiled or egg-fried rice.

Variations
Use beef or lamb in place of the pork. Use swede or turnips in place of the carrots. Use garlic in place of the ginger.

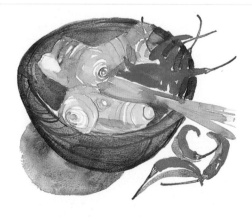

Braised Belly of Pork

A fragrantly spiced pork dish, ideal served with boiled rice or egg noodles.

Preparation time: 55 minutes • Cooking time: 30 minutes • Serves: 4-6

Ingredients

1 kg (2 lb 4 oz) belly of pork	*30 ml (2 tbsp) sugar*
90 ml (6 tbsp) vegetable oil	*250 ml (9 fl oz) rice wine*
2 pieces star or Chinese anise	*2.5 ml (½ tsp) salt*
500 ml (18 fl oz) meat stock	*50 g (1¾ oz) spring onions, sliced*
85 g (3 oz) sweet bean paste	*into 5-cm (2-inch) lengths*
75 ml (2½ fl oz) light soy sauce	*15 ml (1 tbsp) sesame oil*

Method

1

Wash the belly of pork under cold running water, pat dry with absorbent kitchen paper, then remove and discard the bones. Cook the pork in a large saucepan of simmering water, then remove and place in cold water for about 30 minutes. Drain, dry and slice the pork into bite-sized pieces.

2

Heat the vegetable oil in a wok and stir-fry the star or Chinese anise for 30 seconds. Add the stock, sweet bean paste, soy sauce, sugar, rice wine and salt and stir together. Stir-fry for 5 minutes.

3

Add the pork, reduce the heat and stir-fry for about 20 minutes before increasing the heat to reduce the sauce.

4

Add the spring onions and sesame oil and stir-fry for 1 minute. Serve hot.

Serving suggestion
Serve with boiled rice or noodles, or egg-fried rice.

Variations
Use sesame oil in place of the vegetable oil. Use dry sherry in place of the rice wine.

Five-Spice Pork

Serve this spicy-hot yet sweet pork dish with boiled rice.

Preparation time: 10 minutes • Cooking time: 15 minutes

Ingredients

For the Red Curry Paste
(makes 45-60 ml/3-4 tbsp):

12 small red chillies, chopped	700 g (1 lb 9 oz) belly of pork slices
3 cloves garlic, crushed	30 ml (2 tbsp) groundnut oil
1 stem lemon grass, chopped	15 ml (1 tbsp) Red Curry Paste
1 small onion, finely chopped	30 ml (2 tbsp) fish sauce
5 ml (1 tsp) grated root ginger	15 ml (1 tbsp) light soy sauce
10 ml (2 tsp) chopped coriander stems	30 ml (2 tbsp) sugar
A large pinch of ground cumin	5 ml (1 tsp) five-spice powder
5 ml (1 tsp) shrimp paste	15 ml (1 tbsp) chopped lemon grass
30 ml (2 tbsp) vegetable oil	Fresh coriander and lime twists, to garnish

Method

1
To make the Red Curry Paste, place the chillies, garlic, lemon grass and onion in a mortar and pound
with a pestle until the mixture is well bruised and the juices begin to blend.

2
Add all the remaining ingredients except the oil and continue to pound until a paste is formed. Finally, blend in the oil

3
Cut the pork strips into 4-cm (1½-inch) pieces and set aside.

4
Heat the oil in a wok, add the curry paste and stir-fry for 2 minutes. Stir in the fish sauce, soy sauce, sugar,
five-spice powder and lemon grass and stir-fry for a further 3 minutes.

5
Add the pork to the wok and cook, stirring frequently, for 10 minutes, or until the pork is cooked through.

6
Serve hot garnished with fresh coriander and lime twists.

Serving suggestion
Serve with boiled rice.

Variations
Use beef or lamb in place of the pork.

Liver with Mangetout

An inventive way to serve liver, and a quick and easy dish to prepare and cook. You can use pig's, lamb's or calf's liver in this recipe.

Preparation time: 15 minutes, plus 15 minutes marinating time • Cooking time: 5 minutes • Serves: 4

Ingredients

400 g (14 oz) pig's, lamb's or calf's liver	10 g (¼ oz) finely chopped root ginger
15 ml (1 tbsp) potato flour	
10 ml (2 tsp) light soy sauce	**For the sauce:**
5 ml (1 tsp) rice wine	45 ml (3 tbsp) dark soy sauce
75 ml (5 tbsp) groundnut oil	15 ml (1 tbsp) Sha-Cha-Jiang sauce
200-g (7-oz) can water chestnuts, drained and sliced	5 ml (1 tsp) rice wine
150 g (5½ oz) mangetout, trimmed	2.5 ml (½ tsp) sugar
500 ml (18 fl oz) vegetable oil	2 pinches of ground white pepper
75 ml (5 tbsp) sesame oil	7.5 ml (1½ tsp) cornflour

Method

1
Wash the liver under cold running water and pat dry with absorbent kitchen paper. Remove and discard any outer membrane, then thinly slice the liver. Set aside.

2
In a bowl, mix together the potato flour with 30 ml (2 tbsp) water, light soy sauce, rice wine and groundnut oil. Add the liver, stir to mix, then set aside to marinate for 15 minutes.

3
Meanwhile, place the water chestnuts and mangetout in a bowl of cold water for about 15 minutes. Drain thoroughly and pat dry with absorbent kitchen paper.

4
Heat the vegetable oil in a wok, add the liver and cook for about 1 minute. Remove the liver, drain and set aside. Transfer the oil to a suitable heatproof container and set aside. Heat the sesame oil in the wok, add the ginger, water chestnuts and mangetout and stir-fry for 1 minute.

5
For the sauce, in a bowl, mix together the dark soy sauce, Sha-Cha-Jiang sauce, wine, sugar and pepper. Add to the wok with the liver and stir-fry for about 1 minute, until the liver is cooked and tender.

6
Mix the cornflour with 75 ml (5 tbsp) water, add to the wok and stir-fry until thickened. Serve hot.

Serving suggestion
Serve with fragrant rice and a mixed leaf salad.

Variations
Use sugar-snap peas or sliced mushrooms in place of the mangetout.

Cook's tip
Sha-Cha-Jiang sauce is available from Oriental food stores.

Beef with Peppers and Pineapple

Lean beef, red and green peppers and spring onions combine beautifully with pineapple in this tasty stir-fry.

Preparation time: 10 minutes, plus 10 minutes marinating time • Cooking time: 8-10 minutes • Serves: 2-4

Ingredients

250 g (9 oz) beef steak	2.5 ml (½ tsp) freshly ground black pepper
30 ml (2 tbsp) potato flour	500 ml (18 fl oz) vegetable oil
75 ml (5 tbsp), plus 120 ml (8 tbsp) groundnut oil	100 g (3½ oz) red and green peppers, seeded and sliced
20 ml (4 tsp) sesame oil	
15 ml (1 tbsp) sugar	200-g (7-oz) can pineapple cubes, drained
60 ml (4 tbsp) rice vinegar	55 g (2 oz) spring onions, chopped
5 ml (1 tsp) salt	200 ml (7 fl oz) chicken stock

Method

1

Wash the beef under cold running water, pat dry with absorbent kitchen paper, then cut into thin slices.
In a bowl, mix 15 ml (1 tbsp) of the potato flour with 30 ml (2 tbsp) water and 75 ml (5 tbsp) groundnut oil.
Add the beef, stir to mix, then set aside to marinate for 10 minutes.

2

Mix the remaining flour in a bowl with 90 ml (6 tbsp) water, sesame oil, sugar, vinegar, salt and black pepper. Set aside.

3

Heat the vegetable oil in a wok, add the beef and fry for about 1 minute. Remove and keep hot.
Add the peppers and pineapple to the wok and fry for a further 1 minute.

4

Remove from the wok with a slotted spoon, place on a plate and keep hot. Set aside.

5

Transfer the oil to a suitable heatproof container and set aside. Heat the remaining 120 ml (8 tbsp) groundnut oil in the wok,
add the spring onions, peppers and pineapple and stir-fry over a high heat for 1 minute.

6

Return the beef to the wok with the stock and marinade and stir-fry for about 2-3 minutes. Stir in the potato
flour mixture to bind the sauce. Stir-fry until hot and thickened. Serve immediately.

Serving suggestion
Serve with boiled rice or egg noodles.

Variations
Use lamb or pork in place of the beef. Use fresh pineapple in place of canned pineapple.

Spicy Minced Beef

This hot and spicy dish comes from Northern Thailand. Remove the seeds from the chillies and reduce their quantity for a milder alternative.

Preparation time: 10 minutes • Cooking time: 15-20 minutes • Serves: 4

Ingredients

15 ml (1 tbsp) glutinous rice	450 g (1 lb) lean minced beef
15 ml (1 tbsp) groundnut oil	Juice of 1 lemon
1 stem lemon grass, sliced	30 ml (2 tbsp) fish sauce
4 small red chillies, sliced	15 ml (1 tbsp) chopped coriander leaves
2 cloves garlic chopped	Lime wedges, to garnish
15 ml (1 tbsp) grated root ginger	

Method

1

Place the rice in a wok and dry-fry for 5-10 minutes, until the grains are golden on all sides, shaking the wok as it cooks.

2

Pour the toasted rice into a mortar and pound with a pestle until ground almost to a powder.

3

Heat the oil in the wok, add the lemon grass, chillies, garlic and ginger and stir-fry for 3 minutes.

4

Add the beef and stir-fry until the meat changes colour, breaking it up as it cooks.

5

When the beef is cooked, sprinkle with lemon juice and fish sauce. Stir in the ground rice and stir-fry for 1 minute.

6

Transfer to a serving dish, scatter with the chopped coriander leaves and garnish with lime wedges. Serve hot.

Serving suggestion

Serve with mixed stir-fried vegetables and boiled rice or noodles.

Variations

Use minced lamb or pork in place of the beef. Use lime juice in place of the lemon juice.

Cook's tip

If you do not have a pestle and mortar, place the toasted rice in a plastic bag and crush with a rolling pin.

Shredded Beef with Vegetables

A chilli-hot stir-fried beef dish with celery, carrots and leek. To vary the dish, use your own selection of fresh vegetables in season.

Preparation time: 15 minutes • Cooking time: 10 minutes • Serves: 4

Ingredients

225 g (8 oz) lean beef steak, cut into thin strips	1 leek, white part only, cut into thin 5-cm (2-inch) strips
2.5 ml (½ tsp) salt	2 cloves garlic, finely chopped
60 ml (4 tbsp) vegetable oil	5 ml (1 tsp) light soy sauce
1 red and 1 green chilli, cut in half, seeded and sliced into strips	5 ml (1 tsp) dark soy sauce
5 ml (1 tsp) vinegar	10 ml (2 tsp) rice wine or dry sherry
1 stick celery, cut into thin 5-cm (2-inch) strips	5 ml (1 tsp) caster sugar
2 carrots, cut into thin 5-cm (2-inch) strips	2.5 ml (½ tsp) freshly ground black pepper

Method

1
Place the strips of beef in a large bowl and sprinkle with the salt. Rub the salt into the meat and set aside to stand for 5 minutes.

2
Heat 15 ml (1 tbsp) of the oil in a wok. When the oil begins to smoke, reduce the heat and stir in the beef and chillies. Stir-fry for 4-5 minutes.

3
Add the remaining oil and continue stir-frying the beef until crisp.

4
Add the vinegar and stir-fry until it evaporates, then add the celery, carrots, leek and garlic. Stir-fry for 2 minutes.

5
In a small bowl, mix together the soy sauces, wine or sherry, sugar and black pepper.
Pour over the beef and stir-fry for 2 minutes. Serve immediately.

Serving suggestion
Serve with boiled rice and prawn crackers.

Variation
Use chicken, pork or lamb in place of the beef.

Cook's tip
Great care should be taken when preparing fresh chillies. Try not to get juice into the eyes or mouth.
If this should happen, rinse thoroughly with cold water.

Spiced Beef

An aromatic and spicy, quick and easy Chinese-style dish.

Preparation time: 10 minutes, plus 20 minutes marinating time • Cooking time: 6 minutes • Serves: 4

Ingredients

450 g (1 lb) beef fillet	*2.5 ml (½ tsp) salt*
5 ml (1 tsp) soft brown sugar	*30 ml (2 tbsp) vegetable oil*
2-3 star anise, ground	*6 spring onions, sliced*
2.5 ml (½ tsp) ground fennel	*15 ml (1 tbsp) light soy sauce*
15 ml (1 tbsp) dark soy sauce	*2.5 ml (½ tsp) freshly ground black pepper*
2.5-cm (1-inch) piece root ginger, peeled and grated	

Method

1

Cut the beef into thin strips about 2.5-cm (1-inch) long. Set aside.

2

In a bowl, mix together the sugar, spices and dark soy sauce.

3

Add the beef, ginger and salt to the soy sauce mixture and stir well to coat evenly.
Cover and set aside to marinate for 20 minutes.

4

Heat the oil in a wok, add the spring onions and stir-fry for 1 minute.

5

Add the beef and stir-fry for 4 minutes, or until the meat is well browned.

6

Stir in the light soy sauce and black pepper and cool gently for a further 1 minute, stirring occasionally. Serve hot.

Serving suggestion

Serve the beef with a spicy dip and egg-fried rice.

Variation

Add 115 g (4 oz) sliced button mushrooms and 225 g (8 oz) cooked Chinese egg noodles for a change.

Sichuan Meatballs

Sichuan is a region of China that lends its name to a style of cooking which includes many spices, most notably ginger.

Preparation time: 20 minutes • Cooking time: 40 minutes • Serves: 4

Ingredients

85 g (3 oz) blanched almonds	Vegetable oil, for frying
450 g (1 lb) minced beef	45 ml (3 tbsp) dark soy sauce
5 ml (1 tsp) grated root ginger	125 ml (4 fl oz) vegetable stock
1 clove garlic, crushed	15 ml (1 tbsp) rice wine or white wine vinegar
1/2 large green pepper, seeded and chopped	10 ml (2 tsp) honey
	15 ml (1 tbsp) dry sherry
A dash of Sichuan sauce	15 ml (1 tbsp) cornflour
30 ml (2 tbsp) light soy sauce	4 spring onions, sliced diagonally

Method

1
Spread the almonds evenly out on a grill pan and grill under a low heat for 3-4 minutes, or until lightly toasted. Stir the almonds frequently to prevent them from burning. Chop the almonds coarsely using a large sharp knife.

2
In a large bowl, combine the chopped almonds with the mince, ginger, garlic, green pepper, Sichuan sauce and light soy sauce until well blended.

3
Divide the mixture into 16 equal portions and roll each piece into a ball on a lightly floured board.

4
Heat a little oil in a wok and add about half the meatballs in a single layer.

5
Cook the meatballs over a low heat for about 20 minutes, turning them frequently, until they are well browned all over.

6
Transfer to a serving dish and keep warm while you cook the remaining meatballs. Set aside as before.

7
Stir the dark soy sauce, stock and wine or wine vinegar into the wok and bring to the boil.
Boil briskly for about 30 seconds. Add the honey and stir until dissolved.

8
Blend the sherry and cornflour together in a small bowl and add to the hot sauce. Cook, stirring continuously, until thickened.

9
Arrange the meatballs on a serving dish and sprinkle with the spring onions. Pour the sauce over and serve immediately.

Serving suggestion
Serve with boiled rice and a fresh tomato salad.

Variations
Use turkey or chicken mince in place of the beef. Use hazelnuts or brazil nuts in place of the almonds.

Cook's tip
The uncooked meatballs can be frozen for up to 3 months. The sauce should be freshly prepared when required.

Bean Curd with Mushrooms and Spinach

A delicious vegetarian dish of quick-fried bean curd (tofu) and mushrooms served on a bed of freshly cooked spinach.

Preparation time: 15 minutes • Cooking time: 20 minutes • Serves: 4

Ingredients

300 g (10½ oz) bean curd (tofu)	*250 ml (9 fl oz) vegetable stock*
125 g (4½ oz) mushrooms	*30 ml (2 tbsp) dark soy sauce*
200 g (7 oz) spinach	*15 ml (1 tbsp) caster sugar*
45 ml (3 tbsp) groundnut oil	*2.5 m (½ tsp) salt*
A pinch of soft brown sugar	*5 ml (1 tsp) potato flour*
75 ml (5 tbsp) vegetable oil	*45 ml (3 tbsp) sesame oil*
22.5 ml (1½ tbsp) Sha-Cha-Jiang sauce	

Method

1

Cut the bean curd into 2-cm (¾-inch) cubes and set aside. Wipe the mushrooms clean, cut into thin slices and set aside. Remove the stalks of the spinach and discard, then wash the leaves thoroughly. Briefly blanch in a little hot water in a wok, then remove and set aside.

2

Heat the groundnut oil in the wok, add the spinach and soft brown sugar and stir-fry for 1 minute. Remove with a slotted spoon, place on a plate and keep hot.

3

Heat the vegetable oil in the wok and add the Sha-Cha Jiang sauce, stock, bean curd and mushrooms. Reduce the heat and stir-fry for 5-6 minutes. Add the dark soy sauce, caster sugar, salt, potato flour and sesame oil and stir-fry until hot and thickened. Serve the bean curd on a bed of cooked spinach.

Serving suggestion
Serve with jasmine rice.

Variation
Use courgettes in place of the mushrooms.

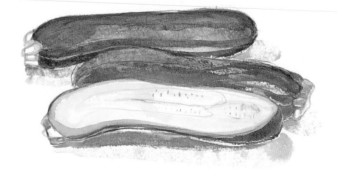

Braised Pumpkin with Aubergines

An unusual vegetable dish which makes a satisfying vegetarian main course.

Preparation time: 10 minutes • Cooking time: 25-35 minutes • Serves: 4

Ingredients

200 g (7 oz) aubergines	37.5 ml (2½ tbsp) sugar
500 g (1 lb 2 oz) pumpkin	7.5 ml (1½ tsp) salt
90 ml (6 tbsp) groundnut oil	A pinch of freshly ground black pepper
3 cloves garlic, finely chopped	
500 ml (18 fl oz) vegetable stock	45 ml (3 tbsp) sesame oil

Method

1

Prepare and wash the aubergines. Cut into triangular pieces and set aside. Peel the pumpkin, remove the seeds and cut the flesh into slices. Set aside.

2

Heat the groundnut oil in a hot wok, add the garlic and aubergines and stir-fry for 2 minutes. Add the pumpkin and stir-fry for a further 1 minute.

3

Add the vegetable stock, bring to a simmer and cook over a medium heat for 20-30 minutes, stirring occasionally. Add the sugar, salt and pepper, then cook for a further 3 minutes over a higher heat to reduce the sauce, stirring frequently.

4

Serve hot with sesame oil drizzled over the aubergines and pumpkin.

Serving suggestion

Serve with boiled rice, pasta or crusty bread.

Variations

Use squash in place of the pumpkin. Use courgettes or marrow in place of the aubergines.

Onion Pancake with Coconut Sauce

An exotic onion-flavoured rice cake fried in the wok and topped with a creamy coconut sauce.

Preparation time: 15 minutes • Cooking time: 15 minutes • Serves: 2-4

Ingredients

350 g (12 oz) onions	*375 ml (13 fl oz) coconut milk*
45 ml (3 tbsp) cooked risotto rice	*30 ml (2 tbsp) tomato ketchup*
120 ml (8 tbsp) plain flour	*7.5 ml (1½ tsp) sambal oelek*
A pinch of salt, plus 2.5 ml (½ tsp)	*1.25 ml (¼ tsp) ground white pepper*
2.5 ml (½ tsp) sugar	*150 ml (10 tbsp) vegetable oil*
30 ml (2 tbsp) groundnut oil	*250 g (1 oz) spring onions, sliced into strips*

Method

1

Peel the onions and chop into small pieces. Place in a bowl with the cooked risotto rice, flour, 125 ml (4 fl oz) water, the pinch of salt, sugar and groundnut oil. Mix well and set aside.

2

For the sauce, in a bowl mix together the coconut milk, tomato ketchup, sambal oelek, the remaining salt and white pepper and set aside.

3

Heat 75 ml (5 tbsp) of the vegetable oil in a wok. Pour half the rice and onion mixture into the wok to cover the bottom of the wok evenly. Cook both sides of the pancake for about 5 minutes. Remove, place on a plate and keep hot. Repeat with the other half of the mixture. Remove and keep hot.

4

Heat the remaining vegetable oil in the wok and add the spring onions and sauce mixture. Stir-fry for 2 minutes. Pour the sauce over the pancakes to serve.

Serving suggestion
Serve with stir-fried mixed vegetables.

Variations
Use leeks in place of the onions. Use cooked brown rice in place of the risotto rice.

Cook's tip
Canned coconut milk is available from many supermarkets as well as Oriental food stores. Stir the contents of the can together before using.

Stir-Fried Baby Corn with Mushrooms

A flavourful Thai-style side dish which is very quick and easy to prepare.

Preparation time: 10 minutes • Cooking time: 8-10 minutes • Serves: 4

Ingredients

30 ml (2 tbsp) vegetable oil	225-g (8-oz) can straw mushrooms
2 cloves garlic, crushed	15 ml (1 tbsp) grated galangal
4 shallots, chopped	2.5 ml (½ tsp) dried chilli flakes
450 g (1 lb) baby corn cobs, cut in half lengthways	15 ml (1 tbsp) fish sauce
115 g (4 oz) mangetout	15 ml (1 tbsp) soy sauce

Method

1

Heat the oil in a wok, add the garlic and shallots and stir until softened.

2

Add the baby corn cobs and stir-fry for 5 minutes, then add the mangetout and stir-fry for a further 2 minutes.

3

Stir in the mushrooms, galangal and chilli flakes and stir-fry for 2 minutes. Sprinkle with the fish and soy sauces and serve immediately.

Serving suggestion

Serve with grilled lean meat or fish and boiled rice or noodles.

Variations

Use 1 onion in place of the shallots. Use baby courgettes in place of the baby corn cobs.

Cook's tip

Galangal is similar in appearance to root ginger but has a milder, more perfumed flavour. Used in the same way as ginger, it is available fresh or dried from Oriental food stores. If you cannot find it, use ginger in its place.

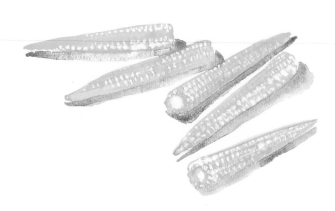

Vegetable Stir-Fry with Bean Curd

Bean curd (tofu) is an excellent source of protein for vegetarian meals. Added to stir-fried mixed vegetables, as in this recipe, it makes a substantial supper dish.

Preparation time: 15 minutes • Cooking time: 8-10 minutes • Serves: 4

Ingredients

50 ml (2 fl oz) vegetable oil	50 ml (2 fl oz) soy sauce
25 g (1 oz) blanched whole almonds	5 ml (1 tsp) sesame oil
4 spears broccoli, cut into florets and stalks sliced	5 ml (1 tsp) dry sherry
115 g (4 oz) baby corn cobs, cut in half lengthways	150 ml (¼ pint) vegetable stock
	10 ml (2 tsp) cornflour
1 clove garlic, crushed	115 g (4 oz) bean sprouts
1 red pepper, seeded and thinly sliced	4 spring onions, cut into thin diagonal slices
115 g (4 oz) mangetout	225 g (8 oz) bean curd (tofu), cut into small dice
55 g (2 oz) water chestnuts, thinly sliced	Salt and freshly ground black pepper

Method

1

Heat the oil in a wok. Add the almonds and stir-fry until they are golden brown.
Remove the almonds from the wok and set aside.

2

Add the sliced broccoli stalks and corn cobs to the wok and stir-fry for 1-2 minutes.

3

Add the garlic, red pepper, mangetout, water chestnuts and the broccoli florets. Stir-fry for 1-2 minutes.

4

In a small bowl or jug, mix together the soy sauce, sesame oil, sherry, stock and cornflour until smooth and well blended.

5

Pour the cornflour mixture over the vegetables and stir-fry for 1-2 minutes, until thickened and hot.

6

Add the bean sprouts, browned almonds, spring onions and bean curd. Stir-fry for 1-2 minutes, until piping hot.

7

Season to taste with salt and pepper and serve at once.

Serving suggestion
Serve with boiled rice or mixed grains and seeds.

Variations
Use any combination of fresh vegetables in season. Use smoked bean curd (tofu) in place of the ordinary bean curd.

Stir-Fried Beans and Sprouts

This stir-fry makes a high-fibre meal and, being partly microwaved, it is easy to prepare.

Preparation time: 45 minutes • Cooking time: 8 minutes

Ingredients

225 g (8 oz) dried adzuki beans, soaked overnight in water	*1 large green pepper, seeded and cut into thin strips*
15 ml (1 tbsp) soya oil	*225 g (8 oz) bean sprouts*
1 large onion, thickly sliced	*600 ml (4 tbsp) soy sauce*

Method

1

Drain the beans and place in a large bowl. Cover the beans with boiling water, then cover the bowl with cling film and pierce several times with the tip of a sharp knife.

2

Cook the beans in a microwave oven on HIGH for 10 minutes, reduce the power setting to MEDIUM and cook for a further 30 minutes, or until the beans are soft and completely cooked.

3

Drain the beans and rinse in cold water. Leave in a colander to drain completely.

4

Heat the oil in a wok. Add the onion and pepper and stir-fry for 2-3 minutes.

5

Add the bean sprouts and stir-fry for a further 1 minute.

6

Add the cooked beans and soy sauce to the vegetables and stir-fry for 3-4 minutes, until cooked and piping hot. Serve immediately.

Serving suggestion

Serve with boiled brown or white rice.

Variations

Use red or yellow peppers in place of the green pepper.

Cook's tip

Great care must be taken when rehydrating beans. The beans must be well soaked and completely cooked before being eaten.

Ginger Cauliflower

This is a simple and subtly flavoured vegetable dish, delicately spiced with ginger.

Preparation time: 10 minutes • Cooking time: 15 minutes • Serves: 4

Ingredients

45 ml (3 tbsp) vegetable oil	*1 medium cauliflower, cut into 2.5-cm (1-inch) florets*
2.5-cm (1-inch) piece root ginger, peeled and sliced	*Salt, to taste*
	2-3 sprigs fresh coriander, chopped
1-2 green chillies, cut in half lengthways	*Juice of 1 lemon*

Method

1
Heat the oil in a wok, add the onion, ginger and chillies and stir-fry over a high heat for 2-3 minutes.

2
Add the cauliflower and salt. Stir to mix well.

3
Cover and cook over a low heat for 5-6 minutes, stirring occasionally.

4
Add the chopped coriander and cook for a further 2-3 minutes, or until the cauliflower florets are just tender, stirring frequently.

5
Sprinkle with the lemon juice, mix well and serve immediately.

Serving suggestion
Serve with wholemeal pitta bread and a fresh tomato salad

Variations
Use broccoli in place of the cauliflower. Use sesame oil in place of the vegetable oil.

Cook's tip
Leaving the chilli seeds in will produce a very hot dish. Remove the seeds for a milder flavour.

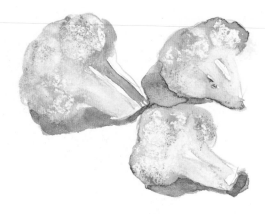

Chinese Leaf Chicken Stir-Fry Salad

This is a delicious, warm salad which is substantial enough to serve as a main course.

Preparation time: 15 minutes • Cooking time: 15 minutes • Serves: 4

Ingredients

60 ml (4 tbsp) olive oil	*1 green pepper, cut into thin 5-cm (1-inch) strips*
3 cloves garlic, crushed	*2 sticks celery, cut into thin 5-cm (2-inch) strips*
450 g (1 lb) chicken breast, skinned and cut into 1-cm (½-in) wide strips	*15 ml (1 tbsp) chopped parsley*
225 g (8 oz) Chinese leaves, shredded	*30-45 ml (2-3 tbsp) dry vermouth*
½ cucumber, cut into thin 5-cm (2-inch) strips	*Salt and freshly ground pepper*

Method

1

Heat 45 ml (3 tbsp) of the oil in a wok and stir-fry the garlic and chicken over a medium high heat for 10 minutes, or until tender and lightly browned but cooked through. Remove the chicken and keep hot.

2

Add the Chinese leaves, cucumber, pepper and celery to the wok with the remaining oil and stir-fry for 2-3 minutes.

3

Place the mixture onto a heated serving dish or individual plates, then spoon the chicken on top.

4

Add the parsley and vermouth to the wok and scrape any browned pan juices from the bottom. Season to taste with salt and pepper, pour over the chicken and vegetables and serve at once.

Serving suggestion

Serve with fresh crusty bread.

Variations

Use courgettes in place of the cucumber. Use turkey or pork in place of the chicken.

Mixed Vegetable Stir-Fried Salad

An appetising combination of fresh stir-fried vegetables, full of texture and flavour.

Preparation time: 15 minutes • Cooking time: 10 minutes • Serves: 4

Ingredients

1 onion	*225 g (8 oz) mangetout, trimmed*
2 large leeks	*115 g (4 oz) bean sprouts or lentil sprouts*
60 ml (4 tbsp) olive oil	*Salt and freshly ground black pepper*
2 cloves garlic, crushed	*15 ml (1 tbsp) chopped fresh coriander*

Method

1

Peel the onion and cut into thin rings. Set aside.

2

Trim the leeks and cut down the length of one side. Open the leeks out and wash thoroughly under running water.
Cut each leek into three pieces, then thinly slice each piece lengthways into thin strips. Set aside.

3

Heat the oil in a wok and add the onion and garlic. Stir-fry for 2 minutes, until the onion has softened but not browned.

4

Add the mangetout and sliced leeks and continue stir-frying for 4 minutes.

5

Add the remaining ingredients and stir-fry for a further 2 minutes. Serve piping hot.

Serving suggestion

Serve with boiled rice and sprinkle liberally with soy sauce.

Variation

Use red onion in place of standard onion.

Cook's tip

Sprout your own beans or lentils by putting them into a glass jar, rinse thoroughly and pour in fresh water each day. Cover the
jar opening with muslin and stand on a sunny windowsill. After 3-4 days, the beans or lentils will have sprouted.

Noodles with Pork and Beef

A colourful noodle dish containing a mixture of meats and fresh vegetables.

Preparation time: 20 minutes, plus 10 minutes marinating time • Cooking time: 8-10 minutes • Serves: 2

Ingredients

150 g (5½ oz) egg noodles	500 ml (18 fl oz) vegetable oil
45 ml (3 tbsp) groundnut oil	90 ml (6 tbsp) soya oil
50 g (1¾ oz) beef	30 ml (2 tbsp) oyster sauce
50 g (1¾ oz) pork	30 ml (2 tbsp) soy sauce
22.5 ml (1½ tbsp) potato flour	10 ml (2 tsp) sugar
30 ml (2 tbsp) beaten egg whites	2.5 ml (½ tsp) salt
20 g (¾ oz) dried Sichuan vegetables, soaked and drained	2 pinches of ground white pepper
50 g (1¾ oz) Chinese cabbage	5 ml (1 tsp) sesame oil
20 g (¾ oz) carrots	30 ml (2 tbsp) spring onions, finely chopped

Method

1

Cook the noodles in a saucepan of boiling water until soft, then drain and stir in 15 ml (1 tbsp) of the groundnut oil. Set aside and keep warm. Rinse the beef and pork under cold running water, then slice into thin strips.

2

Prepare the marinade by mixing together the potato flour, egg whites and the remaining groundnut oil in a bowl. Add the pork and beef and mix well, then set aside to marinate for 10 minutes.

3

Slice the Sichuan vegetables, Chinese cabbage and carrots into strips and set aside.

4

Heat the vegetable oil in a wok, add the marinated meat and stir-fry for 1-2 minutes. Remove with a slotted spoon, place on a plate and set aside.

5

Add the vegetables to the oil, stir fry for 1-2 minutes, then remove, drain and set aside. Pour the oil into a suitable heatproof container and set aside.

6

Heat the soya oil in the wok, then add the noodles, vegetables and meat. Stir in the oyster sauce, soy sauce, sugar, salt and white pepper and stir-fry for 2 minutes. Add sesame oil to taste, garnish with spring onions and serve hot.

Serving suggestion

Serve with a mixed leaf salad.

Variations

Use lamb in place of the beef. Use spinach or chard in place of the Chinese leaves. Use parsnips or swede in place of the carrots.

Pork Chow Mein

This ever popular Chinese-style dish makes an exciting midweek lunch or supper.

Preparation time: 15 minutes, plus 15 minutes marinating time • Cooking time: 20 minutes • Serves: 4

Ingredients

280 g (10 oz) dried egg noodles	1 leek, thinly sliced
15 ml (1 tbsp) rice wine or dry sherry	1 red pepper, seeded and cut into strips
15 ml (1 tbsp) light soy sauce	1 small can bamboo shoots, drained and sliced
5 ml (1 tsp) sugar	
450 g (1 lb) pork fillet, thinly sliced	150 ml (¼ pint) chicken stock
45 ml (3 tbsp) vegetable oil	25 g (1 oz) fresh shelled peas
5 ml (1 tsp) grated root ginger	5 ml (1 tsp) cornflour
1 stick celery, sliced diagonally	Salt and freshly ground black pepper

Method

1

Soak the noodles in hot water for 8 minutes, or as directed on the packet. Rinse in cold water and drain thoroughly.

2

In a large bowl, combine the wine, soy sauce and sugar. Add the pork, mix together thoroughly and set aside to marinate for at least 15 minutes.

3

Heat the oil in a wok and add the ginger, celery and leek. Stir-fry for 2 minutes.

4

Add the red pepper and bamboo shoots and stir-fry for a further 2 minutes.

5

Using a slotted spoon, remove the vegetables from the wok and set aside. Increase the heat and add the pork to the wok, reserving the marinade. Stir-fry the pork over a high heat for 4 minutes, or until cooked through.

6

Return the vegetables to the wok, mixing with the pork. Gradually add the chicken stock, stirring well between additions. Add the peas and cook for 2 minutes.

7

Mix the cornflour to a smooth paste with 15 ml (1 tbsp) water. Add to the marinade sauce and stir well.

8

Add the marinade sauce to the vegetables and pork in the wok. Stir-fry until the sauce is thickened and smooth. Add the noodles and stir all the ingredients together thoroughly until heated through.

9

Season to taste and simmer for 3 minutes, stirring occasionally, before serving hot.

Serving suggestion
Serve with boiled rice and prawn crackers.

Variations
Use beef or chicken in place of the pork. Use sesame oil in place of the vegetable oil.

Shrimp Paste Fried Rice

This is a boldly flavoured rice dish which is best served with steamed fresh vegetables.

Preparation time: 10 minutes • Cooking time: 15 minutes • Serves: 4

Ingredients

30 ml (2 tbsp) vegetable oil	*2 eggs, beaten*
4 cloves garlic, crushed	*4 spring onions, sliced*
2 red chillies, seeded and chopped	*45 ml (3 tbsp) fish sauce*
700 g (1 lb 9 oz) cooked rice	*Fresh coriander leaves, to garnish*
30 ml (2 tbsp) shrimp paste	

Method

1

Heat the oil in a wok, add the dried shrimps and stir-fry for about 30 seconds.
Remove and set aside to drain on absorbent kitchen paper.

2

Add the garlic and chillies to the wok and stir-fry until softened.

3

Add the rice and shrimp paste and stir-fry for 5 minutes, or until heated through.

4

Add the beaten eggs and spring onions and cook over a low heat, stirring, until the egg is cooked. Stir in the fish sauce.

5

To serve, sprinkle with the fried dried shirmps and garnish with fresh coriander leaves. Serve immediately.

Serving suggestion
Serve with vegetables such as steamed bok choy or green beans.

Variation
Use 2 shallots or 1 small leek in place of the spring onions.

Fried Rice with Crab

For this rice dish, use chilled, cooked rice so that it breaks up more readily.

Preparation time: 10 minutes • Cooking time: 10 minutes • Serves: 4

Ingredients

30 ml (2 tbsp) vegetable oil	*2 small red chillies, sliced*
2 eggs, beaten	*175-g (6-oz) can crabmeat, drained and flaked*
2 shallots, chopped	
2 cloves garlic, crushed	*30 ml (2 tbsp) fish sauce*
700 g (1 lb 9 oz) cooked rice	*Lime wedges, to garnish*

Method

1

Heat 15 ml (1 tbsp) of the oil in a wok and add about half the eggs. Swirl to thinly coat the wok and form a thin omelette. Cook until the egg sets, then remove from the wok, place on a plate and set aside. Repeat with the remaining egg.

2

Roll up each omelette, shred thinly, place on a plate and set aside.

3

Heat the remaining oil in the wok, add the shallots and garlic and stir-fry until softened. Add the rice and stir-fry for 2 minutes.

4

Stir in the chillies, crab and fish sauce and stir-fry for 2-3 minutes, or until the rice and crab are piping hot.

5

Toss in the egg strips and serve garnished with lime wedges.

Serving suggestion

Serve as an accompaniment to fish, seafood or chicken Oriental dishes.

Variation

Use canned tuna or salmon in place of the crabmeat.

Shrimp Egg Rice

Serve this dish on its own as a light lunch or as part of a more elaborate Chinese meal.

Preparation time: 20 minutes • Cooking time: 15 minutes • Serves: 6

Ingredients

450 g (1 lb) long-grain rice	1 large onion, chopped
2 eggs	2 cloves garlic, chopped
2.5 ml (½ tsp) salt	115 g (2 oz) fresh shelled peas
60 ml (4 tbsp) groundnut oil	30 ml (2 tbsp) dark soy sauce
2 spring onions, chopped	

Method

1

Wash the rice thoroughly and place in a saucepan. Add enough water to come 2.5 cm (1 inch) above the level of the rice.

2

Bring the rice to the boil, stir once, then reduce the heat. Cover and simmer for 5-7 minutes, or until the liquid has been absorbed.

3

Rinse the rice in cold water and fluff up with a fork, to separate the grains. Set aside.

4

In a bowl, beat the eggs with a pinch of salt. Heat 15 ml (1 tbsp) of the oil in a wok and stir-fry the spring onions and onion until soft but not brown. Pour in the egg and stir gently, until the mixture is set. Remove the egg mixture, place in a bowl and set aside.

5

Heat a further 15 ml (1 tbsp) of the oil, add the garlic, shrimps and peas and stir-fry for 2 minutes. Remove from the wok, place on a plate and set aside.

6

Heat the remaining oil in the wok and stir in the rice and remaining salt. Stir-fry until the rice is heated through, then add the egg and shrimp mixtures and the soy sauce, stirring to blend thoroughly. Serve immediately.

Serving suggestion
Serve with prawn crackers and a dark leaf salad.

Variations
Use chopped red peppers or sweetcorn kernels in place of the peas. Use prawns in place of the shrimps.

Cook's tip
Rice can be cooked and frozen up to 6 weeks. Frozen rice should be defrosted and rinsed before being used.

Index